First published in the UK by HarperCollins Children's Books in 2008
1 3 5 7 9 10 8 6 4 2
ISBN-13: 978-0-00-728869-4

Printed and bound in Italy
By Rotolito Lombarda

TRANSFORMERS ANIMATED

HarperCollins *Children's Books*

CONTENTS

Meet the Transformers!

Optimus Prime　　　　**Bulkhead**　　　　**Prowl**　　　　**Bumbleb**

Ratchet   Starscream   Megatron

Someone watches them from a secret lab.

It's Megatron, leader of the evil Decepticons! Megatron would do anything to destroy his enemies, the Autobots. He sees the dinosaurs on his monitor and hatches a plan.

"Those dinosaurs will be my new army," Megatron says.

He programs the robot dinosaurs to attack the Autobots! Now the robots are alive. They are dinobots!

Megatron sends the dinobots to find Optimus and his friends. The T. rex spots the Autobots outside Dino-World.

"Cars and trucks bad! Car robots worse!" he growls. The dinobots attack!

The Autobots fight back. Prowl dodges flames from the triceratops.

Ratchet and Bumblebee trade blasts with the giant T. rex.

"Wow, these guys are strong!" says Bumblebee.

But not for long!
The dinobots get back up. Now they are stronger than ever!
"We have to get them off the street," Bulkhead suggests.
"Good idea!" Prime agrees.

The Autobots transform into vehicle mode. They lead the dinobots off the street and into an empty parking lot.

The dinobots start breathing scorching flames at their enemies. The pavement melts.

Optimus Prime gets an idea. "Quick, melt the tar!" he shouts.

The Autobots start firing at the ground. With the dinobots also shooting fire, the tar gets soft.

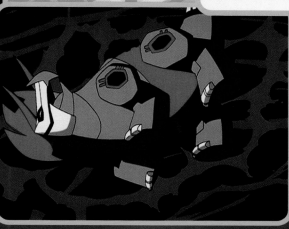

"We need to get them in there," orders Prime.

"I'll take care of it!" offers Bulkhead.

He charges and slams the dinobots into the gooey melted tar.

Now the dinobots are stuck! They can't fight their way out of the tar.

The Autobots saved the day!

"Thank you," Mr Sumdac says to the Autobots later. "I have the dinobots in an energy cage now. That will keep them from causing any more trouble."

"Great," Bumblebee replies. "Maybe now we can enjoy the rest of Dino-World!"

"I think I've had enough dinosaurs for now," says Bulkhead.

The other Autobots laugh.

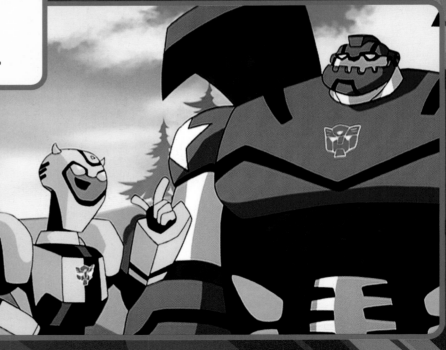

But in his secret lab, Megatron is not amused. "I'll defeat you Autobots yet!" he vows.

MEMORY TEST

1. Where did Optimus Prime, Ratchet, Prowl, Bulkhead and Bumblee visit?

2. Who is the leader of the Decepticons?

3. Who built the robot dinosaurs?

4. What do the dinobots breathe on their enemies?

5. How do the Autobots save the day?

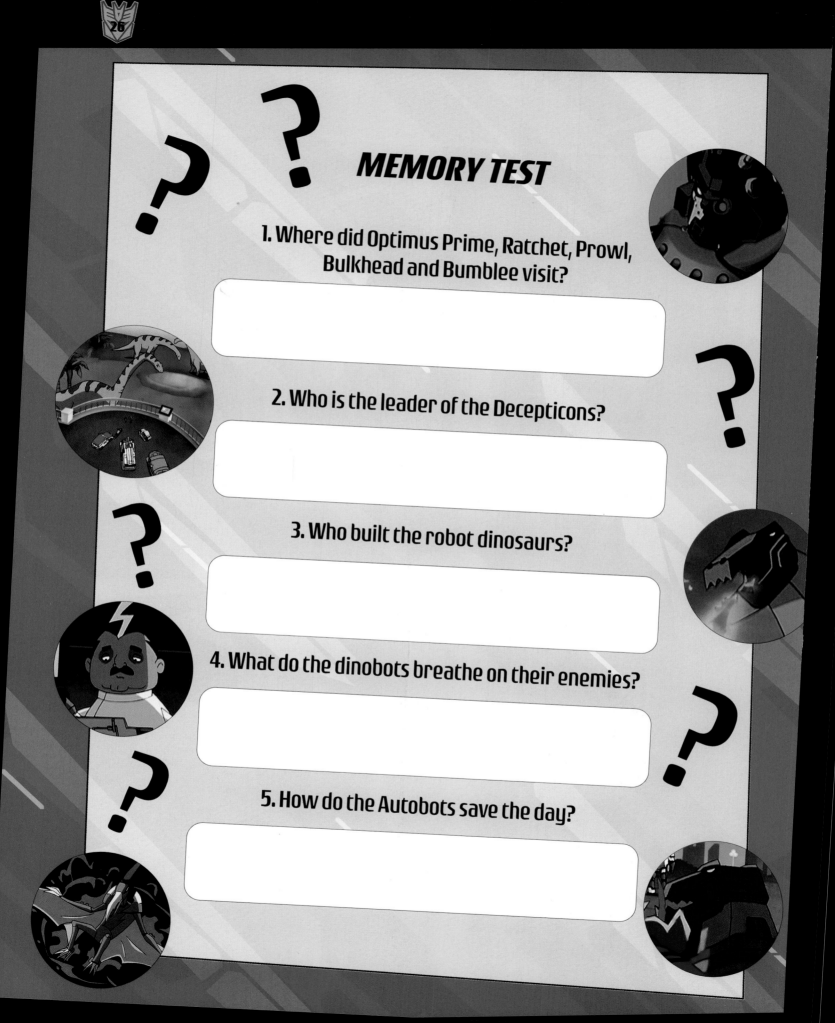

WHO'S WHO?

To fool the Decepticons, Prowl projects holograms of himself.
Can you spot the real Prowl below? Hint: he looks slightly different
from the Prowl holograms.

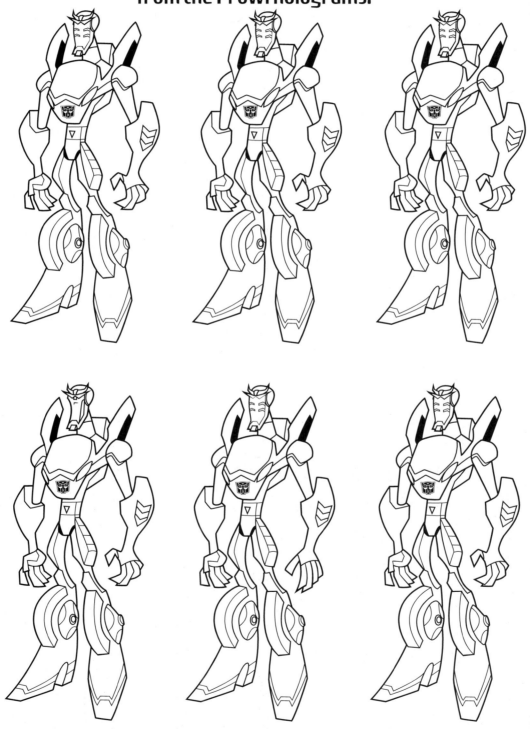

HOME SWEET HOME

The Autobots hope the Allspark will be safe on Earth.
Find the following words in the puzzle below. They will appear forward,
backward, up, down and diagonally.

ALLSPARK	DETROIT	MEGACYCLE
AXE	DRONE	POD
CIRCUIT	FIRE	PROTECT
DAMAGE	KEY	SHURIKEN

A X E E L C Y C A G E M I
F L R M S F K S H P R T S
E S L O S I H E K G P H S
B O M S O M U H I H U M J
F P O D P H O U Z R H X P
Y H P K R A I M I A R S J
E Y P S L K R K B T R U P
K F Y T R L E K K O P X L
D A Z A N N A Q W J P A A
F Q G J N Y T I U C R I C
I W L T D A M A G E N U B
R L C Y C D E T R O I T O
E K D R O N E B U B B I X
T C E T O R P E X J L K L

A CLOSER LOOK

Mr Sumdac builds robots in his lab. Study this picture very closely for one minute. Then turn the page and see how many questions you can answer without flipping back.

Bumblebee

Bumblebee thinks Earth is the place to be.
It's fast, fun and flashy. Just like he is!
Bumblebee is always ready for action.
His stinger blasts can stun anything in his path.

With his super senses and sneaky moves, Prowl can creep up on any enemy. Prowl loves to look at nature. And just like a cat, he is always ready to pounce.

Prowl

THE SPARK OF LIFE

The Allspark is the life source of all Transformers. Long ago,
it disappeared from Optimus Prime's home planet, Cybertron.

How many words can you make from the letters in "CYBERTRON"?

CYBERTRON

_____   _____

_____   _____

_____   _____

_____   _____

_____   _____

_____   _____

_____

_____

WORDS OF WISDOM

Optimus Prime contacts Ultra Magnus on the Comm Screen. Use the decoder to crack the code below and reveal what Ultra Magnus says to Prime.

___ ___ ___ ___ ___ ___ ___ ___ ___
7 10 6 14   14 9 12   14 10

___ ___ ___ ___ ___ ___ ___
5 8 3   4 8 9 10

Decoder:

D = 1+6   H = 11−7   N = 4+2   A = 5−2

R = 16−7   T = 10+4   E = 6+2   B = 1+4

O = 12−2   Y = 6+6

FINDING OPTIMUS...
Check out this image of downtown Detroit.
Can you see where Optimus Prime is hiding?
You have ten seconds to find him!

SPOT THE DIFFERENCE

Can you spot five differences between
these images of Starscream?

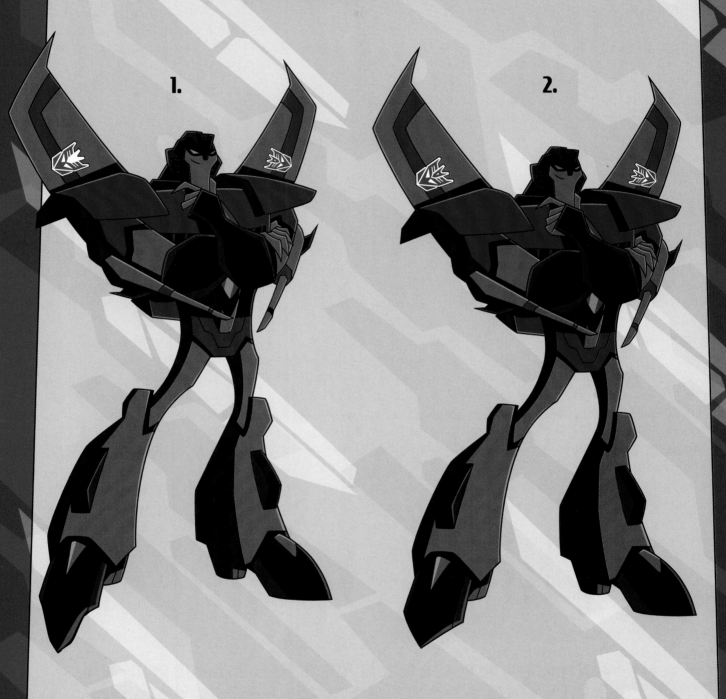

1.

2.

Ratchet

Ratchet is one of the oldest Autobots. He can be gruff and tough, but is always there for a bot in need. Ratchet uses his magnetic powers and medical skills to patch up fallen friends.

Sari Sumdac loves to hang out with her Autobot pals. And her special energy key can heal bots hurt in battle.

Sari Sumdac

Isaac

Sari's dad, Isaac, is a robot scientist.
Busy and curious, his mind is always on his work.

SPEAK UP!

Police Captain Fanzone wants to give orders to the Autobots, but his bullhorn isn't working. Use the decoder below to find out what he has to do to fix his bullhorn.

Decoder:

U =    D =   N =   T =   I =

L =    R =   H = 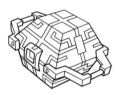   E =   A =

   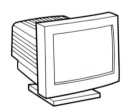   

___   ___   ___   ___

   (continued)

___   ___   ___

___   ___   ___   ___

ARMED AND DANGEROUS

Bulkhead finds Prowl in the rubble.
But he can't find his wrecking ball.
Can you find it hidden in this scene?

MORE THAN MEETS THE EYE

Use the picture clues below to fill out the crossword puzzle.

Down:

 1.

 3.

 4.

 6.

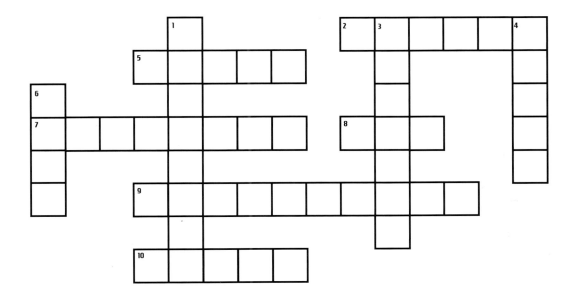

Across:

 2.

 5.

 7.

 8.

 9.

 10.

45

TEAMWORK

Fighting the growing nanobot bug takes brawn and brains. To figure out what Ratchet does to help, unscramble the words below. To finish the sentence, write them in order.

PLESIM   **IDERROVE**   **ANDOMCM**

He creates a

_____   _____   _____

TIME FLIES WHEN YOU'RE HAVING FUN

...with the Autobots!
Circle the four things that are wrong with this picture.

SCHOOL BUS

KEEP AWAY

Can Bumblebee safely pass the Allspark to Bulkhead, or will the Decepticons get their hands on it? Solve the maze to find out!

Start

Finish

MASTER OF DECEPTION

Starscream wants to take out Megatron and become the Decepticon leader. Cross out the word STARSCREAM every time it appears in the puzzle below to find out what he does to Megatron.

```
P S T A R S C R E A M S T A R S C R E A M
S T A R S C R E A M L S T A R S C R E A M
S T A R S C R E A M S T A R S C R E A M A
S T A R S C R E A M S T A R S C R E A M N
T S T A R S C R E A M S T A R S C R E A M
S T A R S C R E A M S S T A R S C R E A M
S T A R S C R E A M A S T A R S C R E A M
S T A R S C R E A M S T A R S C R E A M S
S T A R S C R E A M U S T A R S C R E A M
R S T A R S C R E A M S T A R S C R E A M
S T A R S C R E A M S T A R S C R E A M G
S T A R S C R E A M S T A R S C R E A M E
D S T A R S C R E A M S T A R S C R E A M
S T A R S C R E A M E S T A R S C R E A M
V S T A R S C R E A M S T A R S C R E A M
I S T A R S C R E A M S T A R S C R E A M
S T A R S C R E A M S T A R S C R E A M C
S T A R S C R E A M E S T A R S C R E A M
```

_ _ _ _ _ _ _ _ _ _ _ _

_ _ _ _ _ _ .

Megatron

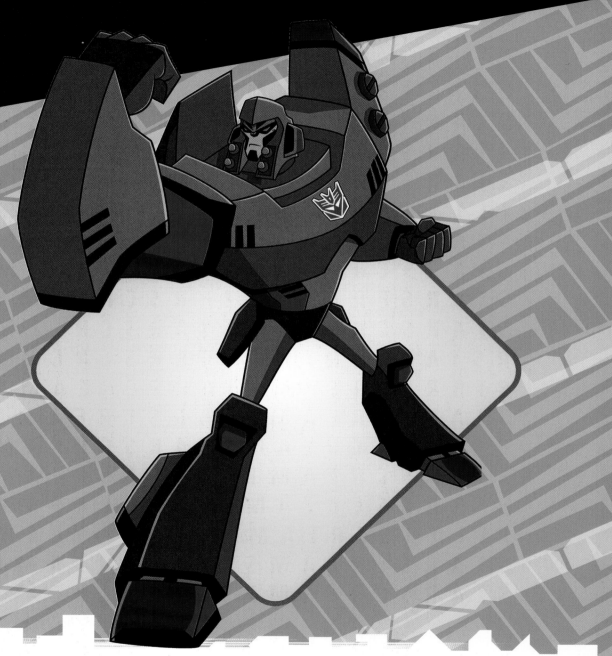

The Autobots are not the only ones new to planet Earth. Megatron is the leader of the Decepticons. He wants to control the Allspark, the source of all energy. First he must stop the Autobots, and anyone else who stands in his way.

Starscream is fast, fierce and full of lies. No one can trust him, not even the other Decepticons. He streaks onto the scene and sends out a supersonic scream.

Starscream

HOW TO DRAW STARSCREAM

In battle, Starscream produces a sonic scream so powerful its sound can send enemies spinning through the air.

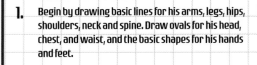

1. Begin by drawing basic lines for his arms, legs, hips, shoulders, neck and spine. Draw ovals for his head, chest, and waist, and the basic shapes for his hands and feet.

2. Give shape to Starscream's body by adding ovals to his arms and legs. His chest and stomach are shaped like an upside-down triangle, with one curved side. Don't forget to add an oval for his neck!

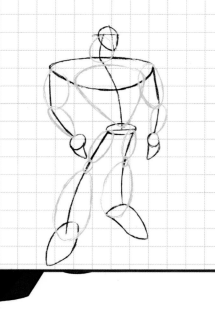

3. Using the ovals as a guide, draw the outline of Starscream's body. Add his thumbs and chin.

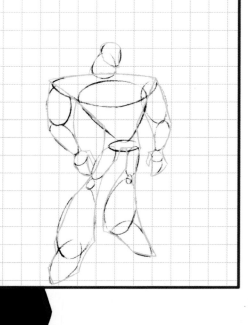

4. Add triangles across his shoulders and the details of his face. Starscream's forearms stick out from his arm, just like his knees stick out from his legs. Draw two intersecting lines across his chest.

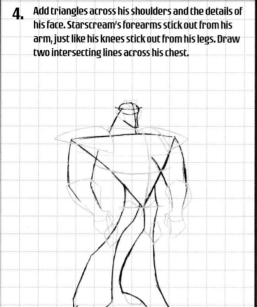

1. To draw Starscream's face, sketch the basic shapes of his head and the guidelines for his features.

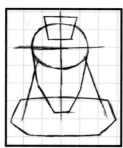

2. Starscream is always scheming. Draw his mischievous expression. His mouth slants toward the left.

3. Add the final details on the sides of his face and top of his head.

5. Draw wings and divide hands into fingers. Add the details on his chest and legs, and blasters on each arm.

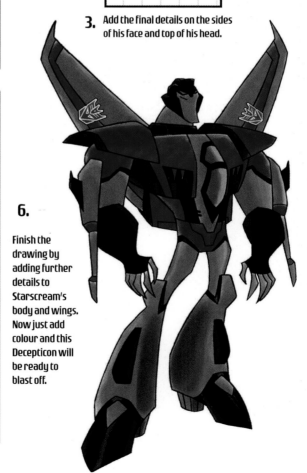

6. Finish the drawing by adding further details to Starscream's body and wings. Now just add colour and this Decepticon will be ready to blast off.

RATCHET'S PUZZLE

Check out these four images of Ratchet.
Can you find the odd one out?

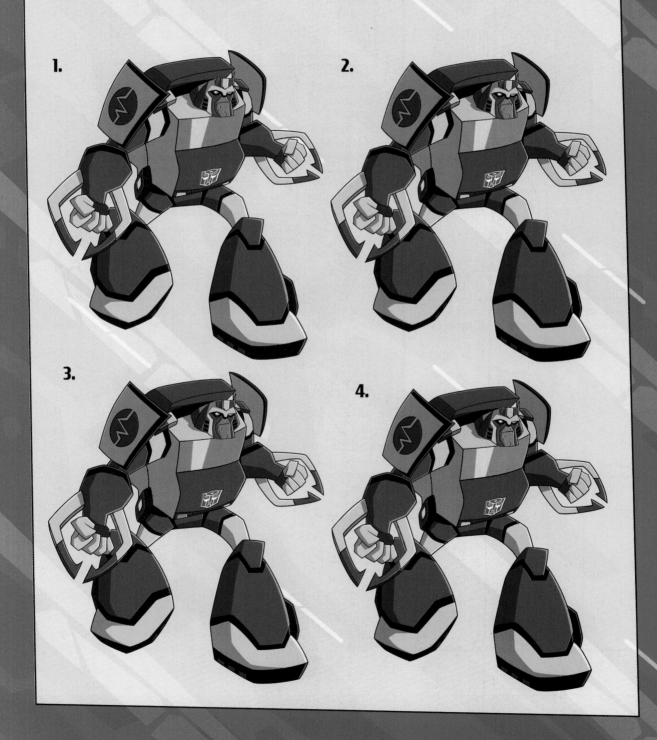

A MAN OF MANY FACES
Circle the three faces that belong to Blitzwing.

HOW TO DRAW THE RACECAR

Bumblebee's secret identity is a small, speeding racecar.
Follow the steps below to disguise this Autobot.

1. Begin by drawing the basic shapes of the car. Add a guideline for the front corner.

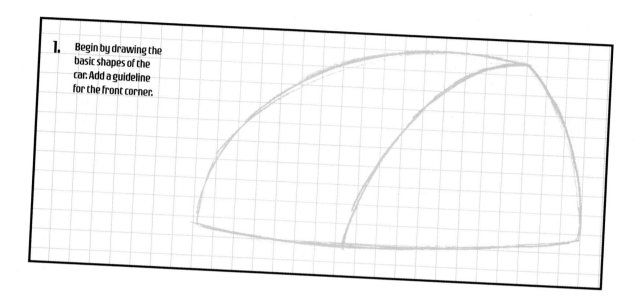

2. Now draw the curved lines that form the windshield and side windows. Add the bumper and two thin ovals for the wheels. Don't forget to add Bumblebee's headlights!

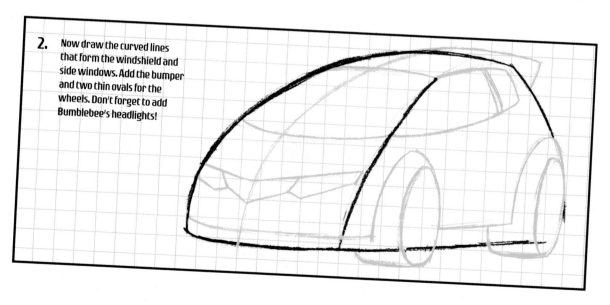

3. To make this car look real, add rearview mirrors and the details on the wheels. Unlike most of the other vehicles, Bumblebee has smooth tyres. Add the detail on the bumper and use three curved lines to draw the light on top.

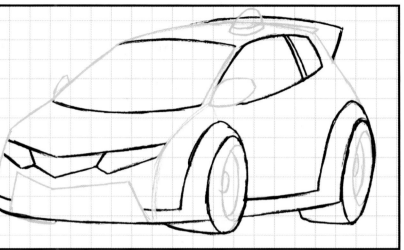

4. Finish your drawing by adding the stripes on the hood and roof of the car and the highlight on the windshield. Finally, draw the details on the bumper, door and tyres.

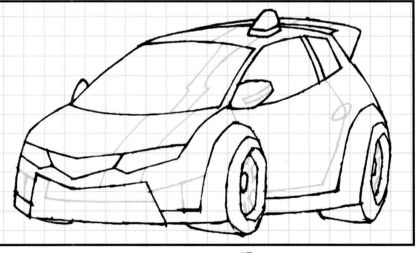

5. Now give this racecar a sleek paint job!

A MAGNETIC PERSONALITY

Ratchet to the rescue! His magnetic field lifts the nanobot
bug creature off Prowl and suspends it in the air.

DISGUISE TIME!

Now it's your turn to be a Transformer! Think of the best Transformer you can and draw your creation in the space below! Remember to include mighty weapons!

ANSWERS

PAGE 26

1. Dino-World
2. Megatron
3. Mr Sumdac
4. Fire
5. They push the Dinobots in melted tar.

PAGE 27

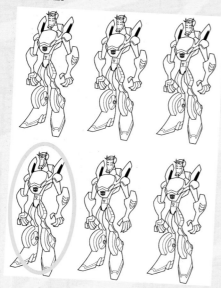

PAGE 28

A X E — E L C Y C A G E M — I
F L R M S F K S H P R T — S
E S L O S I H E K G P H S
B O M S O M U H I H U M J
F P O D P H O U Z R H X P
Y H P K R A I M I A R S J
E K H P P Y S R K R K B T R U P
D F A Z T A L E K K O P X L
F Q G J N N A Q W J P A A
I W L J T Y T I U C R I C
R L C Y C D A M A G E N U B
E K D R O N E B U B B I X
T C E T O R P E X J L K L

PAGE 30

1. TRUE
2. FALSE
3. FALSE
4. TRUE
5. TRUE

PAGE 36

Some of the words you can make are:
be, bent, berry, bet, bore, born, boy, by, bye,
cent, core, corn, corner, cot, cry, ebony, entry,
err, net, nor, not, note, obey, on, once, one, or,
reborn, rent, retry, rob, robe, rot, ten, toe,
ton, tone, tore, torn, toy, try, yen, yet.

PAGE 37

**DONT TRY TO
BE A HERO**

PAGE 38

PAGE 43

PAGE 44

PAGE 39

1.

TURN THE DIAL

PAGE 45

					¹C							²B	R	I	D	G	⁴E
		⁵T	O	W	E	R						³A					A
⁶S					M							T					R
⁷A	L	L	S	P	A	R	K			⁸I	C	Y					T
R					U							H					H
I			⁹S	T	A	R	S	C	R	E	A	M					
					T							E					
		¹⁰T	R	A	I	N						T					

PAGE 48

PAGE 49

PLANTS A SURGE DEVICE.

PAGE 46

SIMPLE   OVERRIDE   COMMAND

PAGE 47

PAGE 54

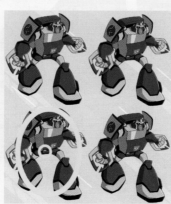

PAGE 55

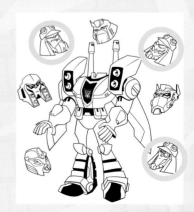